QUEER INSISTS

QUEER INSISTS

(for José Esteban Muñoz[†])

Michael O'Rourke

dead letter office

BABEL Working Group

punctum books ∗ brooklyn, ny

QUEER INSISTS (for José Esteban Muñoz[†])
© Michael O'Rourke, 2014.

First published in 2014 by
dead letter office, BABEL Working Group
an imprint of punctum books
Brooklyn, New York
http://punctumbooks.com

The BABEL Working Group is a collective and desiring-assemblage of scholar-gypsies with no leaders or followers, no top and no bottom, and only a middle. BABEL roams and stalks the ruins of the post-historical university as a multiplicity, a pack, looking for other roaming packs with which to cohabit and build temporary shelters for intellectual vagabonds. We also take in strays.

ISBN-13: 978-0692344736
ISBN-10: 069234473X

Now that José is lost and found, improperly dispersed in us, it's our job to bear that, to be borne by that, to keep being reborn in that. So let's play.

Frederick Moten

Queer Insists

(for José Esteban Muñoz[†])

address delivered at Kenyon College

27 March 2014[1]

---

[1] I wish to thank Laurie Finke for bringing me to Kenyon College to give this address, and I also wish to thank Martin Shichtman and Mary Kate Hurley for traveling a certain distance to see me.

Queer insists (for José Esteban Muñoz). The title is no more than a fragment, little bits, morsels, bites. On December 4, 2013, out of the blue, without warning, suddenly, like a thunder clap, the world learned of the untimely passing of the queer performance scholar José Esteban Muñoz.

///

I never met him personally and saw him speak only once. It was at the Queer Matters conference in London in 2004 where he gave a paper with Jack Halberstam on queer temporality and the "now" of queer studies then. It was a packed auditorium for a star-studded, glitter-glutted plenary session with José, Jack, and Michael Warner. Unsurprisingly, for a talk on queer temporality, José was characteristically late showing up. But his performance was rousing as he breathlessly barked into the microphone. I remember thinking that this was more like a punk rock concert than a polite (even queer studies colloquia tend to be less messy than you would hope) academic event. And this was my first impression of Muñoz, ten years before his death: that he was what I saw myself as being, a rogue theorist. Gustavus Stadler consolidates this impression. He asserts: "Punk rock and its culture galvanized José's way of seeing the world, well before he became an accomplished theorist. Indeed, one could plausibly argue that virtually all of it extends directly from the messy business of being a queer Cuban-born kid on the threshold of a subculture so often oblivious to its racism and homophobia."[2]

///

Even though I had never met him or spoken to him face to face, the loss was felt no less palpably for me that December. It felt like losing Eve Sedgwick all over again and of course Muñoz was Eve's student.

///

I knew I would miss him. Is this counterfeit mourning in the sense that I had never actually met him, studied with him, partied with him? Is it possible to mourn the other with whom one has a relation *only in books*? I wondered about all of this on that dark December day. I felt then that my mourning was what Derrida calls *demi-deuil*,

---

[2] Gustavus Stadler, "Listening, Ephemerality, Queer Fidelity," in Petra Dierkes-Thrun, ed., "José Esteban Muñoz (1967-2013): A Collage," *The b2 Review,* March 10, 2014: http://boundary2.org/2014/03/10/listening-ephem erality-and-queer-fidelity/.

of half-mourning, which would be inter-
able. But Muñoz, in his book *Disidentifica-
ons*, insists on refusing the burden of what he
termed "liveness" as he drew up the plans, "a utopian blueprint," for a "possible future."[3] In a way
then, Muñoz was *always already* a ghost and
queerness for him is insistently hauntological, has
a revenantal structure.

///

If queerness ever showed up, would we even recognize it? (That is one formulation for what
Muñoz's work preoccupied itself with from his
first book *Disidentifications* to *Cruising Utopia*[4]
to his as-yet-unpublished ghost book-to-come,
perhaps posthumographously), *The Sense of
Brown*. If Muñoz ever showed up, and the reflec-
tions of his friends all refer to how he *always
turned up late*, would we even recognize him?

///

I was on a bus just a couple of days after learning

[3] José Esteban Muñoz, *Disidentifications: Queers of
Color and the Performance of Politics* (Minneapolis:
University of Minnesota Press, 1999), 200.
[4] José Esteban Muñoz, *Cruising Utopia: The Then and
There of Queer Futurity* (New York: New York Univer-
sity Press, 2009).

of his passing when the title came to me, "Quee Insists (for José Muñoz)." I was thinking then about how, for Muñoz, queer does not (yet) exist, is horizonal, promissory. Queer does not exist in the here and now; future queerness as we might call it always occupies the ghostly temporality and spatiality of the then and there. Ghosts come from the past and from the future. As Muñoz's death put everything out of joint for me, I noted that the time of queerness is always disjointed, never here, never now. But for all that, queer, as it came to me on the bus that day, insists for Muñoz. The title can, of course, go either way: queer insists for José Muñoz and queer insists, this is an essay *for*, a memorial address *to*, José Muñoz. The insistence of queer. I will come back to this.

///

In my suitcase for this trip I have a copy of Roland Barthes' very beautiful mourning diary for his mother.[5] Barthes asks quite insistently: where is she? Where is *maman*? That is one way of characterizing Barthes' work after the death of his

[5] Roland Barthes, *Mourning Diary: October 26, 1977–September 15, 1979*, trans. Richard Howard (New York: Hill & Wang, 2010).

mother, especially *Camera Lucida*. But the
mourning diary precedes both the texts of *Camera Lucida* and *The Neuter*, both of which he was
working on as he grieved the recent loss of his
mother. The diary itself is a collection of fragments, scraps of paper which Barthes scribbled
on almost every day for a year after her death. It
is a staggeringly beautiful book. And again we
have bits, bites, morsels (and we ought not to
forget that *mors* sounds a lot like *mort*, death in
French). This was the *form*, the fragmentary demand, which insisted itself on me for this talk. If
Muñoz's corpus was marked by a certain unruliness, a spirit of "exuding some rut" by prancing
about on the academic stage, then I resolved to
write a messy text about him, even a para-text or
a peri-text, since what I will have to say here tonight is adjacent to the proper work of mourning,
the tidy essay which would, perhaps, have the
unfortunate consequence of introjecting the lost
other, of having done with mourning once and
for all, as if it were possible.

///

I say that I had never met him but we had corresponded on and off for over a decade. I remember
our first ever email conversation. I had invited
José to be on the board of a new queer studies

journal that, despite having endorsements from Eve Sedgwick, Judith Butler, and Lee Edelman (among many others), never ever got off the ground. It was, and is, a piece of queer ephemera, and, of course, the ephemeral is what interested and animated the work of José Muñoz right from the beginning. I no longer have that email exchange (more loss) because the account closed down (more ephemera). But I do recall—and I have it archived somewhere—a glowing endorsement from him (the punctum as always for me when it came to José was light, luminescence, radiance, a vibrant gaudiness he shared with everyone around him). That was my first of the first encounters with him. I think it was 2002, perhaps—an alternative title would be "Queer *Perhaps* (for José Muñoz)."

///

A longer version of this talk would have to be an irreverent reading of José's books alongside those of John Caputo, especially his most recently published *The Insistence of God: A Theology of Perhaps.*[6] Caputo, like Muñoz, sees "the perhaps" as

[6] John D. Caputo, *The Insistence of God: A Theology of Perhaps* (Bloomington: Indiana University Press, 2013).

the order of a weak thought, a weak ontology of the event, an order of hauntology, a radical opening in and of the present. The perhaps

> prevents the present from closing down upon itself, from being identical with itself, leaving it structurally exposed to the future, not the future present but the very structure of the to-come (*à-venir*). The event (*évenement*) is the advent of what is coming, the coming (*venir*) of what we cannot see coming (*voir venir*), the coming of the future (*l'avenir*) which always comes as a surprise and includes the best and the worst.[7]

The *perhaps* for Caputo, as with queerness for Muñoz, opens thinking to the weak force of the to-come. "Perhaps" is the only way to say yes to the future, Caputo insists. And when Caputo speaks of the insistence of God rather than his existence, he means that "the name of God is an insistent call or solicitation that is visited upon the world, and whether God comes to exist depends upon whether we resist or assist this insistence."[8] For Muñoz, if we substitute "queerness" where Caputo writes "God" (although Caputo's

[7] Caputo, *The Insistence of God*, 5.
[8] Caputo, *The Insistence of God*, 14.

evasia & conspiracy, wrought absence [handwritten annotation]

"perhaps" is always more than a little bit queer), then the insistence of queer would mean Muñoz's insistence on a perverse grammatology or poetics of the perhaps, that queerness insists upon exist-ing. A reading of Caputo alongside Muñoz would finally have to reckon with Caputo's praise for rogues: "I gladly take my stand with the outlaw and ask what theology would look like were it written by the outlaws, the outliers, the out of power, the troublemakers, the poor, the rogues."[9]

///

I have been lucky enough to work with José (what tense should I be using when I talk about him? past? future? future anterior?) three times in the last few years. As an editor for the *Queer Interventions* series at Ashgate Press, I played a part in shepherding through an essay he wrote for a book called *Queer Futures: Reconsidering Ethics, Activism, and the Political.*[10] It is the first major collection to take on the anti-social thesis in queer studies, a dominant position of refusing the future which José's work so resolutely and affirma-

[9] Caputo, *The Insistence of God*, 26.
[10] Elahe Haschemi Yekani, Eveline Killian, and Beatrice Michaelis, eds., *Queer Futures: Reconsidering Ethics, Activism, and the Political* (Farnham, UK: Ashgate, 2013).

tively opposed with its insistence on fashioning
and shaping queer worlds and futures as yet un-
imaginable. In that book José wrote an essay on
Gary Fisher, another student of Eve Sedgwick's
whose poetry she posthumously published in the
book *Gary in your Pocket*.[11] In this essay José insists on the incommensurability of queerness and
on the need for the "sharing of unshareable
thoughts and desires,"[12] as well as upon the
"communing of incommensurable singulari-
ties."[13] In his estimation, the anti-social thesis
freezes or concretizes queer politics, which is, as
he says, barely graspable, ontologizable, or ana-
lyzable. Queer politics is promissory, even rare in
Rancière's sense, and we must have a Badiousian
fidelity to it. He says in that essay (which echoes
the sentiments of *Cruising Utopia*), "I argue that
queerness does not yet exist. I instead offer the
proposition that queerness is an ideality or a fig-

[11] Gary Fisher, *Gary in Your Pocket: Stories and Note-
books of Gary Fisher*, ed. Eve Kosofsky Sedgwick
(Durham: Duke University Press, 1996). The title of
Muñoz's essay in *Queer Futures* is "Race, Sex, and the
Incommensurate: Gary Fisher with Eve Kosofsky
Sedgwick."

[12] Vojin Saša Vukadinović, "Beyond the Political?" in
Yekani, Killian, and Michaelis, eds., *Queer Futures*, 99–
100.

[13] Munoz, "Race, Sex, and the Incommensurate," 112.

uration of a mode of being in the world that is not yet here."[14] He explains that "a queer politics of the incommensurable" or a "queer politics of life" is "most graspable to us as a *sense* rather than as a politics."[15] Queerness is something which is insistently *sensed* (a word which came to replace *feeling* in Muñoz's work). As he proposes it, we need "an understanding of *queerness as a sense of the incalculable*, and, simultaneously, *the incalculable sense of queerness*."[16]

Music, especially punk rock, has a slippery, incalculability that it shares with Muñozian queerness. Gustavus Stadler confirms this sense:

> Events happen and then they're gone. In that recent essay, José invoked Alain Badiou's notion of "fidelity": "We understand and know the event not so much through the moment itself, but instead through the fidelity we have to a transformative spike in our public or personal histories." I think we can infer that this, too, is what a term like "audio fidelity" meant

---

[14] Munoz, "Race, Sex, and the Incommensurate," 103.
[15] Munoz, "Race, Sex, and the Incommensurate," 104.
[16] Munoz, "Race, Sex, and the Incommensurate," 104.

to him—not a set of fixed principles of sonic quality, but a kind of fidelity to the work the medium of sound offered in helping one carry through on the promise of such a "transformative spike."[17]

///

Muñoz's work, in his essay in *Queer Futures*, and elsewhere, presents a profound challenge to the calcifications or entombments of queer theory (I would venture that his death gives us another occasion to ponder the *many deaths* of queer theory and its *many afterlives*, its immemorial currents, even its immortal life). All those terms which, despite its best efforts queer theory has trouble unsettling—the human, identity, politics—are persistently decentered and upended in Muñoz's writing.

///

I notice that he italicizes *sense* and *queerness as a sense of the incalculable.* Just as Derrida always

---

[17] Stadler, "Listening, Ephemerality." The essay of Muñoz that Stadler is referring to is: "'Gimme Gimme This . . . Gimme Gimme That': Annihilation and Innovation in the Punk Rock Commons," *Social Text* 31.3 (2013): 95–110.

italicized the *peut-être* (the *perhaps*). We will come back to this.

///

From *Disidentifications* onwards Muñoz aspired to the making of queer worlds and to the framing of an aspirational politics of "queer world-making" in the form of a "dream work" in which worlds are as palpable as things, in both Michel Serres' sense of "living together" and Lauren Berlant's world-making as a reimagining or reenvisioning of the political in terms of a "lateral exploration of an elsewhere" or *elsewheres*.[18]

///

Last night José Muñoz appeared twice in my own "dream-work." The first encounter seemed to take place in a cinema. He was sitting behind me, in a leather jacket, smiling. I said something about my *sense* of losing him. His response was to laugh loudly and say something in French, which I could not catch even though he repeated it twice. I think it was a quotation from Proust but

[18] Michel Serres, *The Parasite*, trans. Larry Schehr (Baltimore: Johns Hopkins Press, 1982), 224–225; Lauren Berlant, *Cruel Optimism* (Durham: Duke University Press, 2011), 20.

even in the dream-work there is loss. Still smiling he leaned forward in his seat (I guess it is significant that he was behind me and I had to turn to speak to him) and was so close that my nostrils were filled with the smell of his leather coat. Then, unexpectedly, he bit me on the shoulder. Again: the bit, bite, morsel, wound.

///

Much later in the dream Muñoz showed up again. This time we are walking down the street in my hometown, Kells, and the conversation is about an essay I had asked him to write. He confides to me that he regrets not having been able to do it for me at the time. What I gather is that the essay (and this is all imagined) he is talking about comes from his book yet to-come on the sense of brownness and the "brown undercommons." Again he is laughing and says, "if only you had asked me twenty years ago." My reply was that, "I would ask him in my queer future to come." Juana María Rodríguez has written that, "the future queerness of José's intellectual imagination has always been peopled with the still beating hearts of the ghosts of his *chusma* past, those far away from the limelight of the academic stages he graced so ungracefully. Carrying the memory of dreams deferred, and the promise of raucous outrage, he demanded a new formulation of time that could encompass both."[19]

///

The next time we worked together was on an essay he wrote for a collection I am editing on Eve Sedgwick which will now appear posthumously. What I remember most vividly about those email exchanges was his insistence on getting it right. Draft after draft appeared until, finally, he said he was happy.

///

More recently he would be the more than enthusiastic editor for a dossier in *Social Text* on the work of Elizabeth Freeman, especially her book *Time Binds*.[20] He gently chided me for not attending to race and class in the prospectus. As Rodríguez again puts it, "refusing the burden of liveness is about rejecting the restrictive temporality of minoritarian subjects to dwell in the con-

[19] Juana María Rodríguez, "Our *Chusma*, Ourselves: On the Ghosts of Queerness Past," in Dierkes-Thrun, ed., "José Esteban Muñoz (1967-2013): A Collage": http://boundary2.org/2014/03/10/our-chusma-ourselves-on-the-ghosts-of-queerness-past/.

[20] Elizabeth Freeman, *Time Binds: Queer Temporalities, Queer Histories* (Durham: Duke University Press, 2010).

tained chambers of our singular relevance, to call out the ways we precede and exceed the stages of our signification. To name the haunts of our hurts is to envision the pressures and potentialities of being social subjects capable of envisioning future worlds together."[21] Sadly this will also now come into the world after José has left it, time binding indeed.[22]

///

One of my last correspondences with José was about my own book yet-to-come *Queering Speculative Realism*. He messaged me to ask when it would be coming out and I told him that I was still, interminably, working on it. Some while later he wrote again and half-jokingly told me that I should hurry up and finish it because he wanted to teach it to his class. It is a great sadness to me that he will never have read it, taught it, shared it. But beyond, as before death, he is a great inspiration to me when it comes to writing future worlds into existence or into *insistence*.

///

[21] Rodríguez, "Our *Chusma*, Ourselves."
[22] "Time Binds: A Dossier," eds. Michael O'Rourke and Anne Mulhall, *Social Text: Periscope*, July 10, 2014: http://socialtextjournal.org/periscope_topic/time_binds/.

One book with which I am nearly finished is *Rogue Theory*, a collection of my essays (some published, some new) written over the last decade. Despite the fact that I have always considered Muñoz to be the ultimate rogue, *voyou*, heretic, punk, bad boy theorist, it was not until yesterday that I realized the weight of his influence on my own roguish project.

///

In an essay "The Roguish Future of Queer Studies,"[23] originally published in 2006, I appeal to Muñoz and Halberstam's introduction (co-authored with David Eng) to the special issue of *Social Text* that took up the question (no less relevant today) of "What's queer about queer studies now?"[24] Although I had forgotten it until a day ago, it is clear that the roguishness of what they propose is indispensable for me as I try to work out a theory of queer theory's own autoimmunization or interminable self-criticizability. It is

[23] Michael O'Rourke, "The Roguish Future of Queer Studies," *SQS* [Journal of Queer Studies in Finland] 2: 22–47.

[24] David Eng, with Judith Halberstam and José Esteban Muñoz, "What's Queer About Queer Studies Now?" *Social Text* 23.3/4 (Fall/Winter 2005): 1–17.

worth returning to those two moments: my essay (2006) and their issue (2005), but first heard, as I mentioned earlier, in 2004 in London. In asking as they do, "what's queer about queer studies now?" (and we should be aware by "now" that for Muñoz there is no "now" of queer studies, which insistently refuses the burden of its own "liveness," but is no less lively or alive for that), in asking after the state of queer studies then/now, they are, I think, re-assessing queer studies in the same way that Derrida in *Rogues* re-interrogated the syntagm "democracy to-come." What I mean by that is that Muñoz, Halberstam, and Eng are questioning (or opening up to question) the political utility of the term "queer" in ways that suggest that it is not yet presentable, but always deferred, to-come, *khoral*, something we are always putting off until later. They call for, insist upon, *demand* "a renewed queer studies calibrated to a firm understanding of queer as a political metaphor without a fixed referent." This renewed queer studies which would be incalculable, incommensurable, without conditions would insist on a "broadened consideration of the late twentieth century global crises that have configured historical relations among political economies, the geopolitics of war and terror, and national manifestations of sexual, racial and gendered hierarchies."[25] They sought, then, to map out an urgently new political terrain for queer studies that would make it unfaithful or traitorous to the field as it was then, and still unfortunately is imagined today—that is to say, queer studies *in/as* America. Fred Moten is aware of how Muñoz actually does in all his inappropriateness disrupt this field-formation:

> Similarly: to lose, to relinquish or to veer away from—even if within—a given economy of accumulation—José thinks this in relation to, or as a certain disruption of, property, of propriety, of possession and self-possession, of the modes of subjectivity these engender especially in fucked-up, Locke/d down, America. Inappropriateness such as José's—which is his, and his alone, because it is not his, because he gave it to us from wherever he was and gives it to us from wherever he is—remains undefined by the interplay of regulation and accumulation that it induces.[26]

[25] Eng, Halberstam, and Muñoz, "What's Queer About Queer Studies Now?" 1.
[26] Frederick C. Moten, "The Beauty of José Esteban Muñoz," in Dierkes-Thrun, ed., "José Esteban Muñoz (1967-2013): A Collage": http://boundary2.org/2014/03/10/the-beauty-of-jose-esteban-munoz/.

///

As Derrida puts it in his "The University Without Condition," such an unconditional resistance could

> oppose the university to a great number of powers, for example, to state powers (and thus to the power of the nation state and to its phantasm of indivisible sovereignty, which indicates how the university might be in advance not just cosmopolitan, but universal, extending beyond worldwide citizenship and the nation-state in general), to economic powers (to corporations and to national and international capital), to the powers of the media, ideological and religious and cultural powers and so forth—in short, to all the powers that limit democracy-to-come."[27]

Derrida sees deconstruction—as I do queer theory—as a force (albeit a *weak force*, a weak theory in an unfinished world) of resistance and of dissidence (Muñoz might say of disidentification) for

[27] Jacques Derrida, "The University Without Condition," in *Without Alibi*, trans. Peggy Kamuf (Stanford: University of California Press, 2002), 204–205 [202–237].

the new humanities, the humanities to-come in the university without condition. And we might also imagine, as Muñoz does, that queer studies, if it attunes itself to world politics (to critical climate change, financial meltdown, precarity, and so on), could become a space or place—a stage in Muñoz's terms—of "irredentist resistance ... a dissidence in the name of a superior law and a justice of thought."[28] Queer Theory, we could say, and Muñoz would insist on this on behalf of the minoritarian parties, *is* justice, just as this dissidence or resistance is what "puts deconstruction to work or inspires it as justice."[29]

///

Derrida often repeated, no deconstruction without democracy and, in reverse, no democracy without deconstruction, and if we are prepared as Muñoz exhorts us to "to rethink queer critique in relation to a number of historical emergencies, to borrow from Walter Benjamin, of both national and global consequence,"[30] then queer theory just might be a privileged, roguish, delinquent, *roué,*

---

[28] Derrida, "The University Without Condition," 208.
[29] Derrida, "The University Without Condition," 208.
[30] In Eng, Halberstam, and Muñoz, "What's Queer About Queer Studies Now?" 1.

even criminal, countersovereign analytical tool for challenging the powers of sovereign nation states and the "phallo-paterno-philio-fraterno" ipso-centricity of so-called democratic sovereignty.

///

What Muñoz and Derrida are arguing for is a punk commons or rogue undercommons, and in the 2005 *Social Text* issue (cited above), Tavia Nyong'o preliminarily maps what he terms a "punk'd theory," a kind of street theory which would oppose itself to straight theory, by yoking the anti-identitarian referents "punk" and "queer."[31] What I am arguing for—and have been for a long time now—is a "rogue'd theory," where the *voyou* (the rogue) and the queer are etymologically and theoretically (and every other way) entangled. As Derrida tells us, the rogue is always leading astray, seducing, attracting, luring "off the straight path," and pluming himself "like a peacock in rut," and also, "the street is the privileged place of the *roué*, the milieu and the path of the *voyou*, the road most often travelled by rogues, the places they are most often apt to

---

[31] Tavia Nyong'o, "Punk'd Theory," *Social Text* 23.3/4 (Fall/Winter 2005): 19–34.

roam."[32]

///

Muñoz was one such rogue, stray, *roué.* As Rodríguez describes it:

> ... refusing liveness, and forever animated, the performance of Muñozity that erupted whenever José arrived (late of course) was always a happening that he had helped to create and defile before his entrance. Like a *street kid*, passing out flyers to the latest club opening, Muñoz invited everyone to the party, ready to crowd the dance floor of his utopian world-making.[33]

The olfactory dimension of my dream resonates with Rodriguez's description of how "the air would change with the rumor of his presence; it became perfumed with the sticky possibility that there might be enough breathing room for others who were never imagined as belonging, let alone

---

[32] Jacques Derrida, *Rogues: Two Essays on Reason*, trans. Pascale-Anne Brault and Michael Naas (California: Stanford University Press, 2004), 20.

[33] Rodríguez, "Our *Chusma*, Ourselves" (emphasis mine).

worth inhaling."[34]

///

The reaching for a "brown commons" and a "punk rock commons" was also a roguishly relational aspiration. "The challenge here," José writes in an essay on the Los Angeles punk band The Germs, "is to look to queerness as a mode of 'being-with' that defies social conventions and conformism and is innately *heretical* yet still desirous for the world, actively attempting to enact a commons that is not a pulverizing, hierarchical one bequeathed through logics and practices of exploitation."[35] As Jennifer Doyle and Tavia Nyong'o say in the *Artforum* memorial for their friend: "There was something *heretical* about his own work in the academy, the art world, and everything betwixt and beyond them. In making a world for himself in which to flourish, he couldn't help but build one for others too."[36]

///

[34] Rodríguez, "Our *Chusma*, Ourselves."

[35] Muñoz, "'Gimme Gimme This . . . Gimme Gimme That'" (my emphasis).

[36] Jennifer Doyle and Tavia Nyong'o, "José Esteban Muñoz (1967-2013)," *Artforum*, March 14, 2014: http://artforum.com/passages/id=45540 (my emphasis).

In 2005 Muñoz, Halberstam, and Eng were naming such pressing global emergencies for those demanding a new or different order of things as "the triumph of neoliberalism and the collapse of the welfare state, the Bush administration's infinite 'war on terrorism'," and the acute militarization of state violence; the escalation of U.S empire building and the clash of religious fundamentalisms, nationalisms, and patriotisms; the devolution of civil society and the erosion of civil rights; the pathologization of immigrant communities as "terrorist" and racialized populations as "criminal"; the shifting forms of citizenship and migration in a putatively "postidentity" and "postracial" age; the politics of intimacy and the liberal recoding of freedom as secularization, domesticity and marriage; and the return to "moral values" and "family values" as "a prophylactic against political debate, economic redistribution, and cultural dissent."[37] None of these concerns seems any less urgent today. They pointedly begged—as Jack Halberstam does in her recent *Gaga Feminism*[38]—to refocus their political attentions on "public debates about the meaning of democracy

---

[37] Eng, Halberstam, and Muñoz, "What's Queer About Queer Studies Now?" 2.

[38] J. Jack Halberstam, *Gaga Feminism: Sex, Gender, and the End of Normal* (Boston: Beacon Press, 2012).

and freedom, citizenship and immigration, family and community, and the alien and the human in all their national and global manifestations."[39] That urgency is shared by Derrida in *Rogues* where he admits that "in the necessarily finite time of politics and thus of democracy, the democracy to-come certainly does not mean the right to defer, even if it be in the name of some regulative Idea, the experience or even less the injunction of democracy."[40] The bringing into being of roguish queer worlds won't wait—*it insists in the here and now.*

///

Muñoz and the others asked then, what does queer studies have to say about "empire, globalization, neoliberalism, sovereignty, and terrorism?" And even now, with its near exclusive identitarianism and focus on sexuality, the answer would be, *not much.* A roguish queer theory, after Muñoz, would attune itself to these broad social, ethical and political concerns.

///

[39] Eng, Halberstam, and Muñoz, "What's Queer About Queer Studies Now?" 2.
[40] Derrida, *Rogues*, 29.

At the end of their essay "What's Queer About Queer Studies Now?" Eng, Halberstam, and Muñoz suggest that queer studies must produce a politics of "epistemological humility," which means to place ourselves in a vividly "decentered" way in a world "marked by the differences of others."[41] That project—of producing a weak, reparative theory (pace Sedgwick and Butler's Levinasian vulnerability[42])—has not yet been realized. I would suggest, controversially perhaps, that queer theory needs to autoimmunize itself as part of this process of epistemological humility, of decentering and "searching the state of its soul." It needs to resist itself, fold back on itself, in order to resist itself, "inhibit itself in a quasi-autoimmune fashion."[43] Although seemingly paradoxical, it becomes clear that autoimmunity is not only a negative term for Derrida. Indeed it

[41] Eng, Halberstam, and Muñoz, "What's Queer About Queer Studies Now?" 15.

[42] See Eve Kosofsky Sedgwick, "Paranoid Reading and Reparative Reading, or, You're So Paranoid, You Probably Think This Essay Is About You," in *Touching Feeling: Affect, Pedagogy, Performativity* (Durham: Duke University Press, 2003), 123–151, and Judith Butler, *Giving An Account of Oneself* (New York: Fordham University Press, 2005).

[43] Jacques Derrida, "Psychoanalysis Searches the State of its Soul," in Kamuf, trans., *Without Alibi*, 242 [238–280].

opens out to love, to the other. There is a promise of new queer worlds-in-the-making and yet-to-be-made in that threat of autoimmunity—not, as Derrida says, threat and promise by turns, but threat *in* the promise itself. As Derrida suggests, the autoimmune "contradiction" may be constitutive of the democracy or justice to-come, of the emancipatory messianic promise, of Muñoz's queer utopia, of the promise of Queer Studies itself.

///

This opens up, as Muñoz's work on utopia and educated hope supports,[44] the possibility or promise that we might suspend or defer democracy or queer theory, democracy *as* queer theory, for its own good. And the very aporicity of its structure opens queer theory to (again) "taking up its intrinsic plasticity and its interminable self-criticizability, one might even say its interminable analysis." The queer theory to-come, *à venir*, would then, with humility, welcome "in itself, in its very concept, the right to self-critique and per-

[44] In addition to *Cruising Utopia*, see also Muñoz's commentary in Lisa C. Duggan and José Esteban Muñoz, "Hope and Hopelessness: A Dialogue," *Women & Performance: A Journal of Feminist Theory* 19.2 (July 2009): 275–283.

fectibility."[45] This metaperformativity—letting come that which will arrive—frees queer theory, as Muñoz would have it, from any binding teleo-chrono-phenomenology, and it implies, as his later work on punk invoking Badiou's truth procedures does, another thinking of the event: unique, unforeseeable, unmasterable by any ipseity or any conventional or consensual performativity. The queer theory to-come is marked in a to-come that is "beyond the future (since the democratic demand does not wait); it names the coming of *who* comes or of *what* comes to pass, namely the newly arrived whose irruption and arrival should not and cannot be limited by any conditional hospitality on the borders of a policed nation-state."[46]

///

A roguish, unconditionally weak queer studies would open up its borders, render itself porous, even open to the possibility, as Butler might argue, of perhaps "one day abandoning the heritage of inheritance of the name, of changing names."[47] (This might say something to or about Muñoz's

---

[45] Derrida, *Rogues*, 25.
[46] Derrida, *Rogues*, 87.
[47] Derrida, *Rogues*, 89.

changing the title of his last book from *Feeling Brown* to *Sensing Brown*.) This metaperformative, perverse, perverformative, letting come about turns the sovereignties of queer studies against themselves, compromises immunity and lets us know that queer theory *as* democracy is always in the process of immunizing itself. If we are in any doubt as to the positive, deviant, perversely roguish potential of the autoimmune gesture, we should simply listen to Derrida at the end (which is not an end, but another re-beginning) of *Rogues*:

> if an event worthy of this name is to arrive or happen, it must, beyond all mastery, affect a passivity. It must touch an exposed vulnerability, one without absolute immunity, without indemnity; it must touch this vulnerability in its finitude and in a non-horizontal fashion, there where it is not yet or is already no longer possible to face or face up to the unforeseeability of the other. In this regard autoimmunity is not an absolute ill or evil. It enables an exposure to the other, to *what* and to *who* comes—which means that it must remain incalculable. Without autoimmunity, without absolute immunity, nothing would ever happen or arrive; we would no longer wait, await

or expect any event.[48]

///

Jack Halberstam has what we might call an auto-immune reading of losing José Muñoz. He writes that, "some will say that José Esteban Muñoz died an untimely death—he died too young with too much still to do. However, like his formulation of queerness as a state of being that is present in its absence, available as a lost past, unreachable as a beckoning future, I would rather say that Muñoz died as he lived, in a queer time that he may not have chosen but that *insistently* chose him."[49] If queer theory is to be an event worthy of the name, it must, as I have said, suicide itself in an autoimmune gesture which is both a refusal of its own ipso-sovereignty and an opening to, a tym-panization of the future—of who and what will come. Halberstam certainly understands José's death in terms of this promise *in* the threat of death:

[48] Derrida, *Rogues*, 152.
[49] J. Jack Halberstam, "A Leap Into the Void: Finding Muñoz through the Process of Losing Him," in Dier-kes-Thrun, ed., "José Esteban Muñoz (1967-2013): A Collage": http://boundary2.org/2014/03/10/a-leap-into-the-void-finding-munoz-through-the-process-of-losing-him/ (my emphasis).

How might we understand Muñoz's early death through his own work as a gesture of refusal, a refusal of timeliness itself? In "A Jéte out the Window" in *Cruising Utopia*, José writes about the staging of Fred Herko's suicide as his final performance. Using the concept of surplus value to frame acts, work, modes of being which exceed capitalist flows, José uses Herko's leap into the void as an example of an excessive gesture—one that could be read as useless, childish, wasteful, nonsensical—but that literally refuses all that capitalism and capitalist notions of time, offer. Instead, it signals the way in which, within queer aesthetic production, escape and refusal are juxtaposed in an altered temporality that does not respect the markers of "late" and "early" at all.[50]

///

If one had the time you could track references to flight and flying in the responses to Muñoz's death. Kathryn Kent ends her collage piece in *boundary 2* with a reference to Elizabeth Bishop's poem: "In that somewhere, someplace, not yet here, I like to imagine José is waiting, not always

---

[50] Halberstam, "A Leap Into the Void."

so patiently, for the rest of us to, in Bishop's words, 'please come flying'."[51]

///

If, as Rodriguez says, "José was a ghost even before he ever left us," then we might, with Halberstam, read his death as a cruising of the utopian insofar as for Muñoz the utopic—queerness as ideality—cannot be reached through the here and now. (We might remember here that Lee Edelman, before he turned against the future, described queerness or the desire *for* queerness as being utopic in its negativity, asymptotically *curving* endlessly towards the realization that its realization remained impossible.[52]) For Halberstam, Muñoz's sad and sudden exit, his *jeté*, offers us a glimpse of another world beyond the here and now, a "guide to future terrains that may or may not ever surface." And Muñoz's messianicity, inspired more by Ernst Bloch than Derrida, has it that the art of queerness involves "enacting a pre-appearance in the world of another mode of be-

[51] Kathryn R. Kent, "Please Come Flying," in Dierkes-Thrun, ed., "José Esteban Muñoz (1967-2013): A Collage": http://boundary2.org/2014/03/10/please-come-flying/.

[52] Lee Edelman "Queer Theory: Unstating Desire," *GLQ* 2.4 (1995): 343–346.

ing that is not yet here."[53] That not-yet-hereness (as well as an already-goneness) represents perverse temporalities in which *glimpses* of other possibilities and potentialities appear fleetingly.

///   SENSING
                                    & FEELING QUER?

Halberstam interprets Muñoz's last gesture of utopian refusal as an autoimmune act insofar as it turns death, loss, and pain toward the future. Muñoz's last leap is into the unknowable, unforeseeable, incalculable, and absolute vulnerability (which is how, of course, he sees queerness). Halberstam writes that, "if vulnerability is proximity to harm, to unbecoming, then queerness seeks to rewrite the conditions of pain, harm and fear not as identity formations, but as routes to wild embodiment."[54] Queerness, then, is a portal into worlds that Muñoz would describe as fuller, more sensual, brighter, vaster.

///

"Accordingly," Halberstam says, "I do not come to mourn José Esteban Muñoz; I come to celebrate his wild sense of time, possibility, potential-

---

[53] Halberstam, "A Leap Into the Void."
[54] Halberstam, "A Leap Into the Void."

ity."[55] (I am very interested in the tense of that sentence.) In the most oft-cited passage from *Cruising Utopia*, Muñoz writes,

> Queerness is not yet here. Queerness is an ideality. Put another way, we are not yet queer. We may never touch queerness, but we can feel it as the warm illumination of a horizon imbued with potentiality. We have never been queer, yet queerness exists for us as an ideality that can be distilled from the past and used to imagine a future.[56]

Paradoxically, perhaps, we can say that Muñoz's death, as with his life and his writings, makes way for the "warm illumination of the horizon" that we may not now but could in the future to-come see, touch, feel, sense. His death leaves an afterburn (a favourite word of his), or better, an afterglow.

///

A book I forgot to bring with me is Jane Gallop's remarkable *Deaths of the Author*,[57] not death *sin-*

---

[55] Halberstam, "A Leap Into the Void."

[56] Muñoz, *Cruising Utopia*, 1.

[57] Jane Gallop, *Deaths of the Author: Reading and Writ-*

gular as in Barthes, but deaths *plural.* In it Gallop
displays her usual acuity and genius for close
reading. She catches a word, a phrase, a sentence
in her net and spins out a web of interpretation.
Before I had read any memorials for José Muñoz,
the word "insists" had already imposed itself on
me. On 14 March 2014, *boundary 2* published a
"collage" of texts to honor the life and work of
Muñoz written by his friends, colleagues, collabo-
rators.[58] Each is a brief essay, little works of art
each accompanied by a colored rectangle (like an
AIDS quilt, perhaps), which focuses on a specific
idea, passage, or personal memory, and as Petra
Dierkes-Thrun, the curator puts it, it is a "rich
personal collage of love, wonder, grief, apprecia-
tion and admiration for a scholar and a friend
whose work and life will continue to resonate and
inspire beyond his death." I read each of these
short essays with my ear open for the words "insist," "insisted," "insistence," or any of the other –
sistence suffixes (the most obvious being persis-
tence—resonation and inspiration beyond death).

ing in Time (Durham: Duke University Press, 2011).
[58] Petra Dierkes-Thrun, ed., "José Esteban Muñoz
(1967-2013): A Collage," *The b2 Review*, March 14,
2013: http://boundary2.org/2014/03/14/jose-esteban-
munoz-1967-2013-a-collage/.

///

If one had the time, one could perform a reading of each color chosen to accompany the essays in the collage and attend closely to color and colors (greens, browns, pinks) in José's corpus. Beth Freeman, in "Nothing More than Feelings" (her colored rectangle is bright green), imagines a t-shirt with Jose's face imprinted on it:

> Sometime during the days when all the Facebook photos of José with his friends flooded in, José looking at once noble and goofy, fiercely handsome and anime-cute, I had a vision of a T-shirt with a black-and-white, high-contrast picture of José's face. It would echo the Cuban photographer Alberto Korda's famous photo of Che Guevara as made over by Andy Warhol–you know the one. The T-shirt would of course disidentify with Che, capturing and redeploying a certain Latino butchness, a certain solidarity with the freaky people, faggot-style. It would come in turquoise, fuschia, tangerine, sweat yellow, and ACT UP white. [59]

[59] Elizabeth Freeman, "Nothing More Than Feelings," in Dierkes-Thrun, ed., "José Esteban Muñoz (1967-2013): A Collage": http://boundary2.org/2014/03/10/

In her essay titled "Brown Study," Deborah Paredez refers to the day of his death as the blue hour: "it was the *blue* hour and it passed too soon and I was left feeling *brown*."[60]

///

I did have one book in my suitcase that I forgot to take on the journey on from Atlanta to Ohio (this is as much a text about loss and forgetting as anything else; indeed we might, perhaps, understand mourning as "forgetting well" in Derrida's sense of "eating well"). And that book was Hélène Cixous's *Insister*, a book of mourning for Jacques Derrida, one of several books she wrote after his death in order to breathe life back into the texts he wrote, they wrote, he wrote about her, she wrote about him.[61] *Insisting* (being his insister) is a way of halting or interrupting death.

///

nothing-more-than-feelings/.

[60] Deborah Paredez, "Brown Study," in Dierkes-Thrun, ed., "José Esteban Muñoz (1967-2013): A Collage": http://boundary2.org/2014/03/10/brown-study/ (my emphases).

[61] Hélène Cixous, *Insister of Jacques Derrida*, trans. Peggy Kamuf (Stanford: Stanford University Press, 2008).

In the very first essay in the *boundary 2* collage, "Our Chusma, Ourselves: On the Ghosts of Queerness Past," Juana María Rodríguez (who we have heard from already) concludes by writing:

> Even and especially in the stillness of death, he asks us to refuse the burden of liveness, insisting instead that we make the most of *chusma* gestures of ephemera, the trace in the text, the question in the quote, the promise in the queerness yet to come. Having joined the ghosts in the wings throwing shade and brilliance, he invites us—even now—to come out and make a queer production of our broken hearts.[62]

Tellingly, Rodríguez, as Cixous so often does with Derrida, conjures up Muñoz as a "queer child in his Hialeh home" in Cuba (I wonder if after reading this on the plane last night, this is why my second dream encounter with José was in *my* hometown in Ireland …). In concert with Halberstam, Rodríguez seems to understand José's death as an autoimmunitary gesture because it twists and turns queer temporality: "stepping in and out into the ecstasy that exists in another

[62] Rodríguez, "Our *Chusma*, Ourselves."

temporal register where José is about to walk into the room (or was that him who just left?)."[63] *Ekstasis*, a term Muñoz queers and twists from Heidegger (in *Cruising Utopia*), refers both to ecstasy (the drug) and ecstasy (the feeling), an autoimmunity which is partly self-destructive and partly a self-folding outward, a stepping out into another time, another place.

///

We don't have to wait long for more "insistence." In the very next essay in *boundary 2*'s collage "When We Grow Up: Lady Di's Yesterday and José's Tomorrow," Daphne Brooks thinks with the world-that-might-yet-be which the voices of José's friends and interlocutors are keeping alive today, "now." And, like me, she had forgotten how influential, how shaping, Muñoz had been for the landscaping of her own thought:

> If my thoughts about her [Diana Ross] were shaped so wholly and deeply by José Muñoz, the pioneering, field-altering theorist, world-making mentor, institutional-builder and undercommons cartographer, if my thoughts about her *could not* have taken flight without

[63] Rodríguez, "Our *Chusma*, Ourselves."

his *insistence* [my emphasis] on pointing us towards a then-and-there, they were also, unbeknownst to me at the time, holding the kernel of yet another revolutionary manifesto that José was radically improvising already, one that I would hear about the last time I saw him at the American Studies Association: that of "brown theory," an embrace of the here and now and the beauty and power of what we already are.[64]

That work, what she reads in his presence, and writes in his now-absence, is about lady Diana Ross and how she, like José, invites us to elsewheres: "She was always, then, in my childhood, the voice *insisting* that we were as 'normative' as we already were."[65]

///

We have already heard from Halberstam, in "A Leap Into the Void," that it is death which chooses him: "However, like his formulation of queer-

---

[64] Daphne A. Brooks, "When We Grow Up: Lady Di's Yesterday and José's Tomorrow," in Dierkes-Thrun, ed., "José Esteban Muñoz (1967-2013): A Collage": http://boundary2.org/2014/03/10/when-we-grow-up-lady-dis-yesterday-and-joses-tomorrow/.

[65] Brooks, "When We Grow Up" (my emphasis).

ness as a state of being that is present in its absence, available as a lost past, unreachable as a
beckoning future, I would rather say that Muñoz
died as he lived, in a queer time that he may not
have chosen but that *insistently* chose him" (my
emphasis). Muñoz, she feels, sacrifices the here
and now (an autoimmune gesture) for a then and
there that had not yet (prior to his death) and
could not yet arrive. The queerness of (his) death
insists. As Derrida often noted, the worst, includ-
ing death, is what may be to-come, what may
arrive. But there is, as we said, promise in the
threat, and Muñoz's passing should not "dissuade
us from basking in the glow" of that warmly illu-
minated horizon (elsewhere Muñoz himself
would locate this reparativity—as Sedgwick does
too—in the shift from Melanie Klein's paranoid
schizoid position to the depressive position).

///

In "The Realm of Potentiality," Muñoz's friend
Roderick Ferguson writes that,

> Of José Muñoz's inspiring work, the argu-
> ment in which I would most locate and rec-
> ognize my own interests and solidarities would
> be his almost incantatory observation in

Cruising Utopia: The Then and There of Queer Futurity. After calling for a queer politics that dares to "see or imagine the not-yet-conscious," a politics that can derive much of its revolutionary energies from past insurgencies, he wrote, "The not-quite-conscious is the realm of potentiality that must be called on, and *insisted* on, if we are ever to look beyond the pragmatic sphere of the here and now, the hollow nature of the present. Thus, I wish to argue that queerness is not quite here; it is in the language of Italian philosopher Giorgio Agamben, a potentiality.[66]

What draws Ferguson to his work—as it does many of the other contributors to the collage—is that this capacious potentiality is held out to the inexistents, as Badiou would say: "I am drawn to this argument in particular because it is clear that for José a very powerful realm of potentiality—one that can provide us with the resources for the not-quite-conscious, for the utopian future whose materiality we can find in the audacious dreams and visions of past formations—lies in and with

[66] Roderick A. Ferguson, "The Realm of Potentiality," in Dierkes-Thrun, ed., "José Esteban Muñoz (1967-2013): A Collage": http://boundary2.org/2014/03/10/the-realm-of-potentiality-2/ (my emphasis).

minoritized communities and peoples themselves."[67]

///

In "Turning In to *The Sense of Brown*," Ann
Cvetkovich notes that as well as his long-standing
attention to minoritized subjects and communities, Muñoz was a forerunner in what is now go-
ing under the name of affect theory (and no wonder, since he was Eve Sedgwick's student) as he
recalibrates Spivak's famous question as, "how
does the subaltern feel?" Cvetkovich writes (and
this is what, as we know, drew Ferguson to
Muñoz too):

> Even as he is gearing up to explain how Klein-
> ian object-relations theory and the depressive
> position have something to offer, he signals
> the value of ordinary feelings and lived expe-
> rience as a foundation for thinking, as in:
> "Describing the depressive position in rela-
> tion to what I am calling 'brown feeling'
> chronicles a certain ethics of the self that is
> utilized and deployed by people of color and
> other minoritarian subjects who *don't feel
> quite right* within the protocols of normative

[67] Ferguson, "The Realm of Potentiality."

affect and comportment." For those who often "don't feel quite right," this is profoundly enabling work.[68]

Also apparent in the longer passage quoted above is the conceptual challenge of the turn from identity to affect, evident in the rhetorical gestures that underscore this move—the *insistence* that affect is not a mere "placeholder" and the stated desire that it "be something altogether different." By Cvetkovich's lights, Muñoz is an especially hypersensitive reader who tunes and turns in to "receptors" and "frequencies" which allow subalterns to hear, feel and sense, and connect with and to each other. The work of queer world-making and advancing a weak, reparative, messianic theory is precisely about "tuning in" and "turning in" to others. Even more crucially, Cvetkovich claims, Muñoz resists the "whitening" out of affect theory: "His *insistence* that the affective turn be about race needs to be carried forward."[69]

---

[68] Ann Cvetkovich, "Turning In to *The Sense of Brown*," in Dierkes-Thrun, ed., "José Esteban Muñoz (1967-2013): A Collage": http://boundary2.org/2014/03/10/turning-in-to-the-sense-of-brown/.

[69] Cvetkovich, "Turning In to *The Sense of Brown*" (my emphasis).

///

Amy Villarejo's "José's Hope, or what Muñoz Taught" pursues the word "anxiety" in his Bloch-inspired work on hope and hopefulness. She says,

> Stepping out, however, entails, as José knows, risking the imaginative line of a queer horizon. Whether those risks have the name AIDS or other names (disease, drugs, nightlife, travel, poverty, migration, unsafe sex, police …), whether we ecstatically embrace or re*sistingly* [my emphasis] refuse them with all of our energy, they will have enlisted us in our self-definition all the same. Or all the different: the project of *Cruising Utopia* is to offer us an anatomy of queer utopia *as well as disappointment* in many different guises, noticing exactly how potentialities become submerged in recollection, reflection, and other sober *insistences* [my emphasis] upon so-called realism.[70]

In his resistances and ripostes to "so-called realism," we see Muñoz's trademark roguishness and

---

[70] Amy Villarejo, "José's Hope, or what Muñoz Taught," in Dierkes-Thrun, ed., "José Esteban Muñoz (1967-2013): A Collage": http://boundary2.org/2014/03/10/joses-hope-or-what-munoz-taught/.

for Villarejo this is what amounts to his "impertinent reading practice." When Muñoz reads (or writes), he "calls up thunder." That phrase is one I borrow from a poem by Tavia Nyong'o, "For José," written soon after his death,[71] and which is so beautiful that I will read it in its entirety:

For José

José, I'm calling up thunder.

Through so many tears

Today, I'm knocking on your door.

Can you hear?

I'm listening for your laughter through the wall

That separates and connects your office and mine.

I'm eavesdropping for the murmur[72]

of your quiet counsel.

Give me that counsel today.

[71] Tavia Nyong'o, "For José," *Bully Bloggers* [group weblog], December 20, 2013: https://bullybloggers.wordpress.com/2013/12/20/for-jose/.
[72] I cannot help but think of Eve Sedgwick here, E(a)ve (sdropping).

 Gimme, gimme the words,

help me name

what you were to us.

Because there are no words

without you here to help me find them.

José, I'm totally fucked up

In a way that especially you could see.

I'm calling up thunder

for you, for us

for the punk rock commons

whose unauthorized entry

into the Ivory Tower

tooks its stolen wealth

And sold it in the streets for love.

José, you know me:

Most days I go for something pretty

Something pretty and well-spoken

And tomorrow,

I'll say something pretty

but today,

for you José

I'm calling up thunder

to say something true.

///

Many of the responses to José's death have come from musicians and poets. In one memorial essay, "Having a Coke with You: For José Esteban Muñoz (1966-2013)," D. Gilson also calls up an "insistence" in Munoz:

> The day José died, I was working in the lounge of our English department. My mentor, and more importantly, José's friend, Robert McRuer came in and told me on his way to a meeting. I walked down to my own office, stopping to knock on Holly Dugan's door. I cannot—words fail the poet, too—tell you what it felt like to stand in her doorway and think about this mourning together. Holly

and I both adore José, though neither of us knows him well. The mourning of his actual friends on Facebook overshadowed our own feelings, we thought, and rightfully so. Holly and I hugged. She said, *But then again, it shows the power of books, what we're feeling.* We didn't say much. We felt, a cliché I so usually backspace from every poem or essay. I'm a twenty-something hipster, for Christ's sake; one who is not keen on public mourning. But we felt and I think of José and the horizon—

The not-quite-conscious is the realm of potentiality that must be called on, and <u>insisted</u> on, if we are ever to look beyond the pragmatic sphere of the here and now, the hollow nature of the present.[73]

///

I will leave the last "insist" to José himself in an interview from *Bad at Sports*. Asked which contemporary performers best exemplify his idea of

[73] D. Gilson, "Having a Coke With You: For José Esteban Muñoz (1966-2013)," *punctum books* [weblog], December 6, 2013: http://punctumbooks.com/blog/coke-jose-esteban-munoz-1966-2013/ (my underlining).

hope as more than a critical affect for mapping utopias he responds:

> I am interested in so much work that happens under the rich sign of performance. For years I have been following the work of artists like Vaginal Davis whose performances always *insist* on another version of reality than the ones we are bombarded by. I could substitute Vag's name in the previous sentence with that of artists like Nao Bustamente, Carmelita Tropicana, Dynasty Handbag, My Barbarian and so many other artists that I have encountered. I look forward to seeing more work that helps me glimpse something beyond the here and now.[74]

///

Before I finish I want to recall Barbara Browning's "sonnet" written for José:

> when push came to shove, you were all talk,
> all action. that's because you knew to hear

[74] Claudine Ise, "Interview with José Muñoz," *Bad at Sports*, February 7, 2011: http://badatsports.com/2011/interview-with-jose-munoz-author-of-cruising-utopia-and-saic-visiting-artist-lecturer/ (my emphasis).

how portentous a speech act was: the "wow"
and "gee" of it all, the fun of the yack over coke
— let's blow this hamburger stand — better late
than never — you were always late, but somehow
way, like way, ahead of the curve. put jelly
on your shoulder, baby. let us do what
you fear most. it was you who let us feel
this world was not enough, that something was
missing. then you blew the hamburger stand.
hm. thanks a lot. no really. thanks a lot.
no, really. i don't know how to thank you. i think
i may be trying to do it for the rest of my life.[75]

///

José, what I forgot to tell you in my dream last night was that, "I don't know how to thank you either," and I think I may be trying to do that by being a rogue theorist like you for the rest of my life. Thank you.

[75] Barbara Browning, "sonnet," in Dierkes-Thrun, ed., "José Esteban Muñoz (1967-2013): A Collage": http://boundary2.org/2014/03/10/sonnet/.

REFERENCES

Barthes, Roland. *Mourning Diary: October 26, 1977–September 15, 1979*, trans. Richard Howard. New York: Hill & Wang, 2010.

Berlant, Lauren. *Cruel Optimism*. Durham: Duke University Press, 2011.

Brooks, Daphne A. "When We Grow Up: Lady Di's Yesterday and José's Tomorrow." In Dierkes-Thrun, ed., "José Esteban Muñoz (1967-2013): A Collage": http://boundary2.org/2014/03/10/when-we-grow-up-lady-dis-yesterday-and-joses-tomorrow/.

Browning, Barbara. "sonnet." In Dierkes-Thrun, ed., "José Esteban Muñoz (1967-2013): A Collage": http://boundary2.org/2014/03/10/sonnet/.

Butler, Judith. *Giving An Account of Oneself*. New York: Fordham University Press, 2005.

Caputo, John D. *The Insistence of God: A Theolo-*

gy of Perhaps. Bloomington: Indiana University Press, 2013.

Cixous, Hélène. *Insister of Jacques Derrida*, trans. Peggy Kamuf. Stanford: Stanford University Press, 2008.

Cvetkovich, Ann. "Turning In to *The Sense of Brown*," in Dierkes-Thrun, ed., "José Esteban Muñoz (1967-2013): A Collage": http://bound ary2.org/2014/03/10/turning-in-to-the-sense-of -brown/.

Derrida, Jacques. "Psychoanalysis Searches the State of its Soul." In *Without Alibi*, trans. Peggy Kamuf, 238–280. Stanford: Stanford University Press, 2002.

Derrida, Jacques. "The University Without Condition." In *Without Alibi*, trans. Peggy Kamuf, 202–237. Stanford: University of California Press, 2002.

Derrida, Jacques. *Rogues: Two Essays on Reason*, trans. Pascale-Anne Brault and Michael Naas. California: Stanford University Press, 2004.

Dierkes-Thrun, Petra, ed. "José Esteban Muñoz (1967-2013): A Collage," *The b2 Review,* March 10, 2014: http://boundary2.org/2014/03/14/jose -esteban-munoz-1967-2013-a-collage/

Doyle, Jennifer and Tavia Nyong'o. "José Esteban Muñoz (1967-2013)." *Artforum*, March 14, 2014: http://artforum.com/passages/id= 45540.

Duggan, Lisa C. and José Esteban Muñoz. "Hope and Hopelessness: A Dialogue." *Women & Performance: A Journal of Feminist Theory*

19.2 (July 2009): 275–283.

Edelman, Lee. "Queer Theory: Unstating Desire." *GLQ* 2.4 (1995): 343–346.

Eng, David, with Judith Halberstam and José Esteban Muñoz. "What's Queer About Queer Studies Now?" *Social Text* 23.3/4 (Fall/Winter 2005): 1–17.

Ferguson, Roderick A. "The Realm of Potentiality." In Dierkes-Thrun, ed., "José Esteban Muñoz (1967-2013): A Collage": http://boundary2.org/2014/03/10/the-realm-of-potentiality-2/.

Freeman, Elizabeth. *Time Binds: Queer Temporalities, Queer Histories*. Durham: Duke University Press, 2010.

Freeman, Elizabeth. "Nothing More Than Feelings," in Dierkes-Thrun, ed., "José Esteban Muñoz (1967-2013): A Collage": http://boundary2.org/2014/03/10/nothing-more-than- feelings/.

Gallop, Jane. *Deaths of the Author: Reading and Writing in Time*. Durham: Duke University Press, 2011.

Gilson, D. "Having a Coke With You: For José Esteban Muñoz (1966-2013)." *punctum books* [weblog], December 6, 2013: http://punctumbooks.com/blog/coke-jose-esteban-munoz-1966-2013/.

Halberstam, J. Jack. *Gaga Feminism: Sex, Gender, and the End of Normal*. Boston: Beacon Press, 2012.

Halberstam, J. Jack. "A Leap Into the Void: Finding Muñoz through the Process of Losing

Him." In Dierkes-Thrun, ed., "José Esteban
Muñoz (1967-2013): A Collage": http://bound
ary2.org/2014/03/10/a-leap-into-the-void-find
ing-munoz-through-the-process-of-losing-him/.

Ise, Claudine. "Interview with José Muñoz," *Bad
at Sports*, February 7, 2011: http://badatsports.
com/2011/interview-with-jose-munoz-author-of
-cruising-utopia-and-saic-visiting-artist-lectu
urer/.

Kent, Kathryn R. "Please Come Flying." In Dierkes-Thrun, ed., "José Esteban Muñoz (1967-
2013): A Collage": http://boundary2.org/2014
/03/10/please-come-flying.

Moten, Frederick C. "The Beauty of José Esteban
Muñoz," in Dierkes-Thrun, ed., "José Esteban
Muñoz (1967-2013): A Collage": http://boun
dary2.org/2014/03/10/the-beauty-of-jose-esteban
-munoz/.

Muñoz, José Esteban. *Disidentifications: Queers of
Color and the Performance of Politics*. Minneapolis: University of Minnesota Press, 1999.

Muñoz, José Esteban. *Cruising Utopia: The Then
and There of Queer Futurity*. New York: New
York University Press, 2009.

Muñoz, José Esteban. "'Gimme Gimme This . . .
Gimme Gimme That': Annihilation and In-
novation in the Punk Rock Commons." *Social
Text* 31.3 (2013): 95–110.

Nyong'o, Tavia. "Punk'd Theory." *Social Text*
23.3/4 (Fall/Winter 2005): 19–34.

Nyong'o, Tavia. "For José," *Bully Bloggers* [group
weblog], December 20, 2013: https://bullyblog

gers.wordpress.com/2013/12/20/for-jose/.

O'Rourke, Michael. "The Roguish Future of Queer Studies." *SQS* [Journal of Queer Studies in Finland] 2: 22–47.

O'Rourke, Michael and Anne Mulhall, eds. "Time Binds: A Dossier," *Social Text: Periscope*, July 10, 2014: http://socialtextjournal.org/periscope_topic/time_binds/.

Paredez, Deborah. "Brown Study." In Dierkes-Thrun, ed., "José Esteban Muñoz (1967-2013): A Collage": http://boundary2.org/2014/03/10/brown-study/.

Rodríguez, Juana María. "Our *Chusma*, Ourselves: On the Ghosts of Queerness Past." In Dierkes-Thrun, ed., "José Esteban Muñoz (1967-2013): A Collage": http://boundary2.org/2014/03/10/our-chusma-ourselves-on-the-ghosts-of-queerness-past/.

Sedgwick, Eve Kosofsky. "Paranoid Reading and Reparative Reading, or, You're So Paranoid, You Probably Think This Essay Is About You." In *Touching Feeling: Affect, Pedagogy, Performativity*, 123–151. Durham: Duke University Press, 2003.

Serres, Michel. *The Parasite*, trans. Larry Schehr. Baltimore: Johns Hopkins Press, 1982.

Stadler, Gustav. "Listening, Ephemerality, Queer Fidelity." In Dierkes-Thrun, ed., "José Esteban Muñoz (1967-2013): A Collage": http://boundary2.org/2014/03/10/listening-ephemerality-and-queer-fidelity/.

Villarejo, Amy. "José's Hope, or what Muñoz

Taught." In Dierkes-Thrun, ed., "José Esteban
Muñoz (1967-2013): A Collage": http://bound
ary2.org/2014/03/10/joses-hope-or-what-mun
oz-taught/.

Yekani, Elahe Haschemi, Eveline Killian, and
Beatrice Michaelis, eds. *Queer Futures: Recon-
sidering Ethics, Activism, and the Political.*
Farnham, UK: Ashgate, 2013.

W. dreams, like Phaedrus, of an army of thinker-friends, thinker-lovers. He dreams of a thought-army, a thought-pack, which would storm the philosophical Houses of Parliament. He dreams of Tartars from the philosophical steppes, of thought-barbarians, thought-outsiders. What distance would shine in their eyes!

~Lars Iyer

www.babelworkinggroup.org

1967-2013

///

Michael O'Rourke is a postman who lives in Dublin, Ireland. He has published extensively in the areas of Queer Theory, Deconstruction, Speculative Realism, Object Oriented Ontology, Psychoanalysis, Gender and Sexuality Studies, and Feminist Theory. A collection of his essays entitled *Rogue Theory* is forthcoming from punctum books.

///

10343235R00043

Printed in Germany
by Amazon Distribution
GmbH, Leipzig